To RANDY + FRANCIS

Love from
The Nicksons
1/17/03

Stones

A Book of Epigrams

Richard Nickson

Stones
A Book of Epigrams

Published in the United States by Lithic Press
c/o Wishbone 1001 West Washington Boulevard, Chicago, IL 60607

ISBN 0-9663720-0-X
Library of Congress Catalog Card Number: 98-92922

Book design & photography by Markus Greiner & Gregory Nickson.
Photo of poet from "Drumstuck," a film by Gregory Nickson ©1991.
Text layout by Michele Mongello.

Printed by C+D Printshop, Chicago.

To

Guy & Joel
& Gregory

Monuments and stumps of the memorials
are set up of stones; men are stoned
to death; the figurative seed falls in stony places . . . .

—Herman Melville, *Journals,*
on the stones of Judea

CONTENTS

*Any resemblance to real people or events
is wholly intentional.*

I

Eden and After

From the garden's oldest tree
Hangs the evil fruit:
So shall the latest Adam
Steal on errant foot
To reach and pluck and bite it
And live and die a brute
That moralists thereafter
With moralists may dispute.

Lineage

I'm sure he'll have no children,
Neither lass nor lad,
Even as I'm certain
His father never had.

For should his marriage follow
Hereditary laws,
His wife will prove as barren
As ever his mother was.

To a Wealthy Widow

Sweet solace in your loss
Seek, and be glad,
Not for what he was
But what he had.

Savor the recompense
Of mate bereft:
Not just the pile he made
But what he left.

And decked in mourning, take
Your luck in stride:
Not that he ever lived
But that he died.

Second Thought

That oath I swore, *Miranda,*
Never again to call you dense,
Upon reflection finds me
Penitent of my penitence.

The Unswerving

Through all the years *Diane* remains
Steadfast in her heart's desires,
Clutching with gnarled hands the gains
That staunch cupidity acquires.

Dead Reckoning

Old age at last caught up with *Rip*
And found him sadly quaking—
Oh, not at death, but at the cost
Of such an undertaking.

God bless old *Rip*! The debit proved
His courage truly stable:
Although a feeble man, he lived,
And died when he was able.

Caveat

He who repines declines;
He who laughs lasts.

Imp of the Perverse

In crabbèd age and youth,
False as his mincing pride,
When asked to speak the truth,
With his forked tongue he lied.

In brittle youth and age,
True to his native bent,
When told to go to hell,
With all his might he went.

The Silenced Majority

And would you know
The reason why
None speak ill
Of *Doctor Sly*?

While in his care,
Who'd dare deprive him
Of his good name
Must first survive him.

Portrait

Unbearably good, impossibly nice,
Hypocrisy's insufferable tool,
He smiles upon his wit's demise—
A most unprecedented fool.

Justice for All

Fleer with an even hand
Deals every man his due:
Sneers for the false and bad,
Snarls for the good and true.

Painless

When to the dentist he departed,
Fondly with each friend he parted.
Oh, it will hurt! they said. They lied.
There was no pain at all; he died.

Pyrrhic Victory

Escaped from all velleities,
The carnal loop, the neural thread,
And wholly, at long last, to know
Indifference, being dead.

One Way

They crossed that bridge when they got to it,
The one that spans the unplumbed wastes of longing,
And set foot on the opposite bank
Leading down into the blind valley of lost content.

Truth

What we cannot speak about
we must pass over in silence.
                    —Wittgenstein

Silent Partners

Even before I knew she knew I knew,
I half expected to hear her say she'd known,
But nothing that was said so much as what was not
Led us to understand that it was understood.

Piano

Approach with wonder this staid instrument
As fingers upon its inert keys evoke
The steel fragility of Chopin.

Piano Forte

Silent the deafened hall
At hearing *Buffo* strum,
Like Eden after the fall,
Struck, like the keyboard, dumb.

Words to the Unwise

Urgently to all express
A burble of urbanity
Lest even your silence should confess,
Quite as your face, some foolishness.
But never speak your mind, because
The little that is there would see
You judged and damned as speedily
As any sinner ever was.

Your True Name Know

"Doctor," "Your Reverence," "The Honorable"—
All, all quite useless tagged to you, I fear.
A fool by any other name would still be foolish,
And you, if possible, foolisher.

Memo

I told you once, I told you twice.
Ah, but we soliloquize who give advice.

Debutantes' Song

We danced in the Autumn
We sang in the Spring
Made love in the Summer
And Autumn and Spring

We dance now in Winter
Make love and sing
Keeping fit for *next* Summer
And Autumn and Spring

Pastime

They who only seek
To pass the time of day
Will find how swiftly sneak
Time and life away.

Like as Not

Austere the ranks of those who know;
Austerer, those who think they do.

Who Goes There?

Never a man who may not be
An honest friend, good company:
Neither a man who might not be
Your deadliest sworn enemy.

Concord

There is an amity of mind
No distances can sever:
Countries, towns we leave behind
But comrades, never.

Lost and Found

Separated at birth,
Mind combed all ways, the known, the hidden,
Seeking without rest as one lost;
Heart, within its quiet center,
Fixed in stillness, as if unseeking,
The sought way, the lost way, found.

Finale

It is agreed that there shall be
Neither the question nor the answer.
A worthy question answers itself
And an answer is never an answer.

Bequeath the laurel to that man
Who sees the rose and doesn't pluck it.
Bequeath the laurel, and the rose
Will close be wound about it.

The Question

Whether to shake one's fists
And curse the blazing noon
Or lacerate both wrists
And giggle at the moon?

Even in Arcadia . . .

No one would not finally yearn,
In the usual manner, to disappear.

The Circle

Were I standing at death's door,
I'd knock and straightway enter,
Quitting life's circumference
To find its center.

The Enemies

Enemies we were—
We quarreled and we fought.
Man's common fate we share:
We were, and we are not.

Alike, the two of us,
Long buried and long forgot,
Cold and oblivious,
In the dark grave we rot.

Preview

Through the world we seek, only to find
Foreshadows of the groping blind:
Like us, enwound in the fate our due,
With time so brisk, our years so few.

Intimations

The trees give up their ghosts of shadows
And night with its heart-corroding hours
Licks at our mortal wounds, foretelling
The consummation of the worm.

The Unknown

In death we forget at last the world
As in life we forgot the womb.
For whom then do we light the pyre,
For whom do we dig the tomb?

Vignette

Squalor of self-interest
Set in the imperturbable faces,
The important look
Of those who ring life up on registers
And pocket art like bills.

The Lecturer

From what I hear of what he says
Nothing can become
Him quite so much as modesty
Or being stricken dumb
As he insistently explains
How what is is not
And out of the wealth of his ignorance
Adds nothing and nothing to nought.

Students

We try to reap who do not sow.
We learn and learn and never know.

Miniature

A marginal one, aloof, alone,
Disdaining almost to exist,
In his pinched abode on a blind road
Paints *Modicum,* the minimalist.

Looking Askance

Sanctity is the veil worn by the prurient,
And sin is the name they give to their own desires
When they are realized by others.

Looking Back

Old age is getting to know
That things once dreamed about
Have never really happened.

Morning Cityscape

Before the sparrows had had time
To commute to the curbside
Rank on rank of bluecoat pigeons
Were already there on patrol.

Gratitude

Rather than to be known
As one who even knew the man
I'll flout his favors, and his loan—
Let the fool regain it if he can!

Faithful Unto Death:
A Colloquy

Ambition
With this ring in my nose, I thee wed.

The Bitch Goddess
And I am yours, till all your blood is bled.

Fiat

The hero acts and rejoices
Irrespective of introspection.
And anyway, like as not,
The unexamined life is not worth examining.

Take Your Pick

Gourmet said to *Greedy-gut,*
"I eat the finest that comes my way."
"Me too—and everything else,"
Greedy-gut said to *Gourmet.*

Hoodwinked

Once *Bluffer* in his huffing way
Swears his job is done,
Here you will find an unwiped slate
And there, an unturned stone.

Providence and Fate

Our daily bread the lord will give us

•   •   •

Ah, but the boor we have *always* with us

•   •   •

Best

Better than age is youth;
Better to live than die;
But better a dead man's truth
Than youth with a slinking lie.

Both Sides

Death is the jangle of a bell,
The matter of a minute.
Life? Oh, life is all very well—
But there's no future in it.

The Lottery

In the muck of days, as such ways tend,
Seek as we may we'll find no more
A simple justice, a decent end
Than a wise zealot or an ardent whore.

Lithic

In the dead of night a wraith unsleeping lurks
Of the once done, never to be undone
Rued and shame-encumbered deed that lies
Deep in the heart, heavy as stone.

Revelation

That in due time we shall cease,
This of all truths known,
This, this only is
Inescapably our own.

Mausolean Inscription

Forsake, O passerby,
The fret of days
In the loud street,
And enter, if you would share
My calm retreat,
These somber portals.

Rivers: A Triptych

1. At the Rubicon

Weighing the strict edict against the wide vistas of chance,
He formed resolve after daring resolve
Before determining at the last
To wait.

2. At the Lethe

Their arms entwined, their sighs
Rapturously breathed as one,
He sought to speak, but could not speak,
Her name.

3. At the Styx

At the verge of the roiling water
He cowered in doubt and dread—
As one just arrived on the fated strand
Or waiting perhaps to be rowed over?

Revised Version

Genesis 3. 6.

At the first taste of the fruit she liked it
And greedily reached for more,
But he who had got there first had left her
Only the seeds and the core.

The Race

With ardors and limbs entangled,
Dazed celebrants of now
Seize the days and also
All that the nights allow.

Whirled in the wiles of doing
Fleetly as ever they've done,
Again and again they enter
The race all lovers run.

La Ronde

Declining or loving
One man never,
Her heart was ever
The pawn of men.
She lost it in roving
From lover to lover
Over and over
And over again.

From swearing eternal
Devotion to any,
She's beloved by many,
Unknown to few.
I sing the infernal
Sublimity of her—
So false to lover,
To love so true.

Losers Weepers

Felicia in a flush of pleasure
Found her joy but lost her treasure.
Fred, who'd helped her find it, wondered
Why she wept for what he'd plundered.

Hopscotch

Rupert longs to lie with *Kate,*
Who longs to lie with *Jim,*
Whose lover *Tess,* to compensate
Rupert, lies with him.

But *Tess,* unsatisfied with him,
Then lies instead with *Kate,*
Leaving it up at last to *Jim*
Rupert to compensate.

The Old Sweet Song

Ego writing to Amnesia in Lethe:
"Promise you'll love me forever."

To Each His Own

They met, and long thereafter
Each kept what time could not erase:
His memory of her girlish laughter,
Her memory of his foolish face.

The Duel

Invariant he, implacable she
Faced off, closed in, made up, fought on,
Embraced and kissed, and instantly
Before he fairly lost, she won.

Double Negative
Her Deposition

No matter how many times
I've said "I won't," I will,
For often as I've said
"You can't," he fucks me still.

In Praise of Learning

Intellectual
Ladies submit
All for the sexual
Love of it.

Slumber Song

Brief the nights with dreaming sped,
Briefer they seem with you.
Time flies fast when one's abed,
But faster far when two.

Cause and Effect

After the fond kiss, fold hands and sit.
Make love? you ask—why, this is it!
My dear, you lie—the words are hollow.
When lightning flashes will not thunder follow?

Unconditional

His advances are froward,
The skirmish to win:
His one route is onward
With never a rout.
So if she's not going
At length to give in—
In short, he's not given
To going without!

Chauvinist, Male

Two lies there are;
Of all, the worst.
Man is one—
But woman first.

Threnody

A pity how quickly good things pass,
Like splendor in the grass, alas.

Bitter Reaping

Desire that brought Antonius down
And laid fair Dido low
Into the tillage of our wounds
Will dark tares sow.

The Decoyed Mistress

Virginia underwent her first
Analysis and straightway burst
With curiosity to try
Her well-preserved virginity.

Roué Refrain

Monogamy's the poor man's drink
With lures and blighted wishes laced.
Dipping in only the one well
Slakes a thirst but starves the taste.

Modus Vivendi

Between us let there be no trace
Of silent pout or loud protest,
Save only when we wake to face
Another day like all the rest.

Conditional

Pledge the allegiance due me
Quickly with no delay!
Tonight you are all things to me—
All! till the break of day.

Libertine Duo
Inferno

The seven sins we glean
From alpha unto zeta
Nel mezzo del cammin
Di nostra dolce vita.

Carpe Diem

Think not of the past
Or futurity:
Banish the has-been
And the yet-to-be.
That which we once were
We now are not,
That which we shall be
Boggles all thought.

Enjoy what present
Joys allow:
Life is in living,
Time is now!
Even as tomorrow's
Yesterday,
So yesterday's tomorrow
Is today.

All American

The beer all guzzled, he and she
Stripped bare for groping hands to be
Free for a tumble in the grass—
And Johnny Johnson came to pass.

Checkmate

She who could've wouldn't,
So he who would've couldn't.
It isn't that she wasn't
Adamant: They didn't.

Found and Lost

A race to the racer
Is over and done
The moment the race is
Run and won.

So love to the lover
Often is nought
When someone to love is
Found, not sought.

Bounder

You don't love me?
I care not, I,
Who love but only
What you deny.

It's that I love
And will, till you
Grant what I would,
And you won't, do.

Sanctus

The sin of wish alone has proved
How well for sanctity he's fitted:
A rose with all the thorns removed,
It blushes red lest he commit it.

Sex Shelter

In the classroom the susurration of the Sister
Enjoining abstinence;
Linnet wings spent in a vacuum.

Wonder

A thing most wonderful I tell,
Of paradise without a hell:
A woman without any wile
Other than a dimpled smile;
One who is prettier than most
And yet can singularly boast
A modest bearing, and withal
Innocent and virginal;
Never forward; never bold;
A thing of wonder, nine years old.

Sotto Voce

"And I am yours!" the one replied
To the other's "I love you."
But in my heart I knew she lied—
And that I did too.

Connubial

So loving is the wife who climbs
Into my bed each night at nine
That I could almost wish sometimes
This ever loving wife were mine.

The Rub

Not that she told me lies,
But that I believed.
I can forget the deceiver,
Never the deceived.

Descent

Rock-hewn for Shiva and for randy Priapus,
The lingam and the phallus.

For us, in these lesser days,
The flaccid condom.

Eve

Of man's first disobedience
She bore the brunt and more—
Verily, all that he brought to bear
Of love and death she bore.

Don Juan in Decline

Of youth bereft and all its lush delights,
He dwindles to a taper of the flame that was,
Thinking of the long days unwinding from a lifeless coil,
Thinking of the long, the ever lengthening nights.

Nocturne

Remorseless dreams arise and bring
To lonely nights as offering
Far-off echoes to frail ears
Of youthful loves and younger years.

Senex

My dear, as my fewer and fewer hairs
Turn whiter and whiter, I fear
A tender word can only make
Me cup both hands to hear.

Bah! That the golden Olden Time
Holds full sway is not
Quite as I see it, since that time
I've more than half forgot.

Time heals all, say those who know
Nothing about how deep
The festering wounds of years incise
The poor dim wits we keep.

Intermission

Dear, I most willingly would in a minute
Cling yet again as we did,
Did not this laggard shrink from its duty
To do as it was bid.

The Sole Original

Contrition asked of *Sin* the reason why,
Despite his wickedness, no one denied
His precedence in austere theology.
"I was here before you," *Sin* replied.

Obbligato

At the grim last, one truth discover,
Grey beard, lean shanks, bald head:
So long as you let love lead, wan lover,
So long will you be misled.

Shall I Compare Thee?

The bright eyes of the sky, the stars,
Though like her eyes they be,
Are much less bright, I swear, than hers,
But far more bright than she.

Qualification

I take you at your word—
But ah, which one?
Each vow no sooner said
Than quite undone.

In turn I vow, although
Grovelling at your feet,
To speak the truth: In you
My faith is incomplete.

I own, however much
Bare truth wounds:
My admiration for you,
Dear, knows bounds.

Treasure Hunt

What are the wonders I descry
Hidden in her darting look?
—The blue recesses of the sky
Mirrored in a shallow brook.

The Invincible

Passion, beauty may
Fade when youth is gone.
Sex bravely wears away
The last of flesh and bone.

Latest to know decay,
It stays till all is gone,
After the heart is clay,
And love, a stone.

Aphrodite

Borne on the four winds forever
The suppliant voices of men
And their pulsing echoes
Calling calling calling
Your fragrant name

III

This Is Not a "Poem"

Before I press pen to paper
The resolve seizes me
Not to title the poem "Poem."

Requiescat

Strew on him weeds and nettles:
Give the devil his due.
In quiet he reposes—
Ah, would his verse did too!

Ars Poetica

The usual progeny of literary men:
Stillborn bastards of a prostitute pen.

Ars Poetica Update

Make it, like, uh, y'know, *new*, he sd.

The Middle Road

He wrote not a measure
Of song or of sense,
And died without giving
Delight or offense.

Rhetorical Question, Poesy Department

Am I making myself perfectly obscure?

Tribute Money

Walt Whitman, the Right Honorable Candidate praises
    you.
You who have borne much, bear this, too.

Art for Their Sake

This coterie, incestuous grown,
Labors to put forth a worn
Semblance of itself, and be
Midwife to its own stillborn.

Quid Pro Quo

Upheld in either hand the trophies
So long by unctuous *Toady* sought:
Bay leaves from his fellow poets
For the blurbs to their verse he'd brought.

Taking the Measure

The man himself, pretentious
Though but of common mold—
Like the body of his work,
Extensive but shoaled.

William Blake

Seraph-singing Blake,
Demonian, half wild:
Of godlike passionate beauty
And only (posthumous) child.

Robert Burns

O best bard of our northern tongue!

Shelley

As Ariel and Prospero
He soared; the Calibans below,
As soon as the flicker of his fame grew bright,
Turned hooded eyes upon the blinding light.

The Poet

Who is the oddling, sawning boy
Who loved his native fields lifelong
And lifted out of dust and toil
His soaring feelings into song?

Who paltry proudlings, killing scorn,
The gaping maw of poverty
Outfaced, and wracked, with reason gone,
Still kept his spirit with the free?

Who in his wondering sight would take
The all of nature into his care,
The woodlark and the pale primrose,
The vixen and the quirking hare?

John Clare. John Clare. John Clare.

Blurb Over All
(After Williams)

so much depends
upon

a network of friends
and lovers

amid a maze
of blurbs

and interviews
et cetera

Antipodal Poesy Americana

Alongside a barbaric yawp
Over the roofs of the world,
Thoughts of a dry brain
In a dry season:
The native hue of Whitman
Sicklied o'er by the pale cast of Eliot.

Onward, Summer Soldiers!

At home, accommodating verses
Strephon gingerly rehearses;
Abroad, he hurls down imprecations
On hosts of fawning foreign nations.
Which is *Strephon?* What is he?
A dual personality
That all our bards, in league, abet.

With purling *da* and snarling *nyet,*
Behold him single in the field
With courage to submit and yield.
Though bent on seeming, center stage,
A monolithic personage,
He's prone to practice on the sly
A singular duplicity.

Point Counterpoint

*All tosh about foreign languages
  making it difficult.* —Pound

In one man's ideograms may lie
Motes to blur another's eye.

One can but glean the words he knows
In poems, even as in prose.

And one's own native tongue to speak is
Simpler than Provençal or Greek is.

Scriptural

Exploring *Zed's* new novel,
Commended by the best of all possible reviewers,
Is like cozying up to a sober reading of Leviticus.

Prudence is All

He shock the crowd? Not him.
He *flatters* the dovecotes.

Discovery

In a poem,
Or in one line alone,
To meet a stranger
You have always known.

Detour

Madame has traveled far and near,
Madame's read all that *really* matters.
But roads like books may lead nowhere,
And that which broadens sometimes scatters.

Remaindered
(Pre-jet)

A feeble flight of wingless words,
Dear bookseller:
Useless as an aeroplane
Without propeller.

Testament

Lampito for his own lampoon
With modesty (becoming tune!)
Inscribed himself for all futurity
A puerile poet of some obscurity.

The Censor

Of old the bearer of ill tidings
Was straightway swung from a noose.
Why can't I hang the pesky blighter
Before he delivers the news?

Poetic Justice

The Muses with extreme vexation
Damned *Pomposo* with a curse,
Who alone throughout the nation
Sang the praise of his own verse.

To a Lady Who Makes Much of Lines

Vatic, portentous dear,
Your verses strike us dumb
With wonder at the sheer
Flux of effluvium.

Inscription for the Tombstone
of a Captious Critic

After print's fitful fever . . .
Absent thee from asperity awhile.

Inscription for an Errata List

Print's a fine and public place,
But none I think do there erase.

The Marketplace

Whether knowledgeable or not,
Essential it is to *seem* to be—
To seem, or to be seen for what
Small half-wittedness you've got.
For judges, juries all agree
The better part of doing well
In business, medicine, or art
Is how abundantly you sell
To client, patient, devotee
Your reputation and yourself,
While they themselves themselves deceive
With fancied gain but actual loss,
Counting as gold your dreck and dross.

IV

The National Religion

Mammon is the one god
And warfare is his profit.

The Last Refuge

My country—wrong or worse!

Chorus of Vested Interests

Our robbery passes
As enterprise,
And we kill only
On sound advice.

Strictly legal
Is the blood we draw:
We always murder
Within the law.

Recapitulation

"Milton! thou shouldst be living at this hour."
Methinks that if thou wert, thou wouldst take pen
Now to assert infernal circumstance
And satirize the ways of men to men.

Excess Profits Tax

What? And would you haul King Profit down
And set that vandal Taxes on his crown?

Rather exhume the dead—start nunnery brawls—
Clip peacocks' tails—lock stallions in stalls!

The Long March

Rude-footed men have trampled
The fairest flowers of time.
Ay, and I hear them trampling
Still the defoliate remains.

A Man for Malfeasance

His every step a false one,
His only hope a prayer,
He sought to win election
By any means but fair.

Without the ghost of substance,
His candidacy but sought
A bland and winning manner
Of buying or being bought.

A gambler, down on his luck,
He aimed with malicious glee
To wheedle that pliant dupe
Mister Vox Populi.

Voters

The cowed truth and the bludgeoning lie—
Between these alternatives we shuttle.

The Politician

A person of various truths
Who takes not one but many stands,
Each contradictory and none just,
Planted inflexibly on shifting sands.

Prime Loser

His faults countless as vermin,
His virtues decidedly numerable,
Worse in its steady march to worst
Has fixed him in the forefront of the retrograde.

Hic Jacet

Don't dig him a grave,
Dig him a ditch.
Here still lies
A son of a bitch.

Our Father Coughlin

Thy priestly robes, they do not fool:
We see the wolf beneath the wool.
Thy oratory does not bluff:
We see the fool beneath the wolf.

Munich

The seven seas
Drift in to shore
As their peace
In to our war.

The British Religion

Faith in the wisdom that comes with age and the
    ruling class
To nothing
Placed in Mr. Chamberlain's copious ability
To *do* nothing.

Post-Mortem

Was anyone so well debunked
As Neville Chamberlain, defunct?

History

Mounting on leaden wings
This old truth will soar:
It was a fabulous peace,
Broken only by war.

Post-Munich

Have you your goggles, gas-mask, dearie?
Have you adjusted the parachute, chum?
Then power dive for the doomed cities:
Ready the bomb-sight, drop the bomb.

Is it you in the steel-top turret, baby?
Is it me behind the fortified hill?
Come, let us fall in line, and quickly
Level our rifles—shoot to kill!

The Enemy

Know the Enemy, know him well—
Here are some sure ways to tell.
Does he shoot in your direction?
This is clearly a defection.
Does he shout for room to live?
He will take all you can give.
Has he lots to say of race?
Genocide comes on apace.
Is he for equality?
Not for you, and not for me.
Does he know the One True Way?
Take another while you may.

Führer! Duce! Caudillo!

For us the half-truths and the multiple lies
Taught us by leaders who know less and less
Rouse us to choose with loud, exultant cries
Pharaohs to lead us through the wilderness.

Addressed to Certain Poetic Gentlemen Who Advocate the Suspension of Civil Rights

We do not say we wish you dead, sweet bards—
It is unnecessary.
You live. We care not. Our one shame is this:
We are contemporary.

Census
(Wartime)

The total marks
A rising gain
On last year's figure,
It is said.

O count them!
All the millions slain,
The population
Of the dead.

War Memorial

You who live, remember me,
As I can not.
Engraven here you see
Words carved on my behalf,
Who am no more.
Once this you see
And read and pass,
Remember me: I am
A generation's epitaph.

Casualty
(S.I.W.)

This is the dreariest grief
Of all bewept:
To be a man of promise,
And unkept.

Tried Souls

Sensing victory or profit as quite near,
The moguls presently began to fear:
Not so much the possibility of losing
As the vexed impossibility—of choosing.

Questionnaire

Your name, young man?
I have a million names.
Your home?
All lands, this earth.
Your age?
Say I am young, or used to be.
Your trade?
They call it war.
Your plans?
Murder!
And your prospects?
Death.

See No Evil

The guardians of the godly heard
The victims' screams, yet they
With their infallibility chose
To look the other way.

The German Ballot

Since plebiscite election
Crowns any man a king,
A little contraception
Is a dangerous thing.

Axial Epitaph

Here lies Il Duce,
Deutschland's pride.
One nice thing about him
Is—he died.

Diplomacy

Now that at last peace has come
We can give ourselves over wholly to war.

Charity at Home and Abroad

Abroad she casts her eyes, insisting
She'd give her life for those resisting.

At home she shuts them, blindly shielding
Those who keep their wealth by yielding.

Smilin' Through

Somewhere over the rainbow
Every cloud will have a strontium lining,
And there—there at the end of the tunnel
A blinding flash.

Obit in Orbit

O passerby from some far other speck in space,
Grave lessons we would teach, who learned not any.
But mute upon this midden lies the human race,
Vaporized by one last war too many.

Pax Americana

Ours is the harried ease that once
Assailed the Romans in their halls
As rumors coiled round the colonnades
Of rallying Visigoths and Gauls.

Last in the Hearts of His Countrymen

In totting up the final score
We must in truth confess
He might have been conceivably more
But inconceivably less.

Siesta

Stripped in the sun I lay,
A buzzard black wheeled round elate.
All in good time, good buzzard!
Let us wait . . . .

Resolution

Always to work for others' good
And only shirk the things I should
Are my resolves, which if I may
I'll make and keep—some other day.

I, Tiresias . . .
(January 9, 1938)

The world is one year older
The days are getting colder
And they'll make me a soldier
For I am twenty-one

October 16, 1940
(Draft Registration)

On this day I became
Nickson, Joseph Richard
Male   Single
23 Blu   White
Number 2109.

Ego

This is my vanity,
This my bane:
I live in sanity
In a world insane.

Ego II

A little good
In much that's bad:
I am sane
In a world gone mad.

"The Craft So Long to Lerne"

Cursèd these ragged sinews—
They and my five senses all bewailed
As with faltering steps I seek to climb
Rungs of a ladder long since scaled.

Spleen

I got up on the wrong side of my deathbed this
    morning,
I loafed and invited my soul and it didn't come.

Phoenician

I have been born quite often
And died immoderately.
Whether living or dead now I know not,
But that since I *am* I must *be.*

Eremitic

I inscribe myself as one
Who is least lonely when alone.

Uxorial

Steadfast in my solitary sway,
For half a century I have duly grown
Accustomed in the customary way
To live my life with but one wife alone.

J'accuse

Fool, said my Muse to me,
  Look in thy heart, and write.

Inveigh against the world, I would,
With all its peopling of narrow-minded
Bastards who'd trample if they could
Truth till it's botched and blinded.

But how will I choose past any doubt
A culprit, known to me, to cite?
By heeding, from within, the shout:
"Fool, look in thy heart: Indict."

I Count; Therefore I Am

Outstretched and counting my ten toes
I drowse and wake and fall asleep again,
And what I am the devil only knows—
Except that five plus five is ten.

Top Prize

Vine leaves for my hair,
And for my common fare
What but the fatted calf?
But though they tempt and please,
I still prefer to these
The last laugh.

Non Serviam

The religious at grips with all wrongs
Lighten the darkness of our day;
But name me an established religion—
I'll be the recusant to cry "Nay."

1992

My youngest son turns thirty-two!
My grandson starts to walk!
Reverse your gears for *me,* swift years!
Stop, Time! —Balk!

Environmental Blues

The polar bear is padding on thin ice,
The eagle flounders in polluted skies,
The mighty whale in toxic ocean dies,
And I'm not feeling very well myself.

Public Inquiry

For my autobiography, I would be grateful
For any pertinent facts and explanations.

That Shakespeherian Rag

That time of yeeare thou maist in me behold
When all of my extremities are cold.

In me thou seest the twilight of such day
As glimmers in a fog and skulks away.

Byron Remembered

The sun's at high noon, but to my grief
My days are in the withered leaf.

Finis

Now, all the flowers furled
And the green leaves turning,
I in turn am turning,
Stalking my dwindling shadow
Into the darkness leading
To the steep defile of death

Homo Necans
(1917-   )

Born into a world at war,
In young manhood I was armed to kill;
Aged now, I look out upon
A world war-torn, blood-stained still.

The Twentieth Century

Often I have felt the clutch of dread
Imagining myself in earlier times
Because of what I know of all their crimes
And because I know to what those crimes have led.

Now and Then

Since fear grapples my heart when I
Look back upon the past—O how
You unborn will recoil when you
Look back upon this hideous Now.

Lia

When I am no longer I
And you are no longer you
Will someone remember who we were:
You with your mild, resplendent eyes
And I who loved to look in them;
You with your smile that drew me in
To a world in which you lived, and I
Lived with your smile, your eyes, with you.

En sourdine

Silent the lilting voice,
The laughter that charmed our ears,
Lost in these later days,
The gathering of years,
Leaving a memory as of birds
Now fluttering, now flown,
With only a murmur of distant bells
And no sound else.

Processional

Departing, I speak only this
To you who will remain:
You tread the well-worn path I trod
And will not tread again.

The Poet

A native of New Mexico, Richard Nickson has had a varied career that includes four years of Army service during World War II; hotel management; and receiving B.A. and M.A. degrees from the University of North Carolina (Chapel Hill) and a Ph.D. from the University of Southern California. Now professor of English Emeritus of William Paterson University, he lives with his artist wife Lia in a Manhattan loft. Their three sons have in turn, so far, fathered three sons.

Nickson has frequently published articles on modern drama, song, and politics; he has also authored numerous scripts for documentary films. His book of lyrical poems *Staves* (1977) continues to attract musical settings. He has written, with Junius Scales, *Cause at Heart,* published by the University of Georgia Press in 1987. For more than two decades he has served as president of The Bernard Shaw Society and is the editor of its tri-annual journal *The Independent Shavian.*

The Poems

Staves: A Book of Songs by Richard Nickson was hailed by poet Thomas McGrath, in his Introduction, as "A rare, strange book for these times." According to McGrath: "It is hard to miss the skill with which these poems are made–the wit, the grace, the lyricism, the elegance, and the iron of a language that at first glance may appear fragile." Novelist Leonard Michaels has written of *Staves,* "If we listen to these songs, we may learn again how to read, as we should, with our ears. They provide a lovely lesson."

During the two decades since their publication, more than half of the seventy lyric poems of *Staves* have been set to music by a variety of distinguished composers and republished with their musical scores by G. Schirmer, Southern, and Boosey & Hawkes.

Now more than 190 of the epigrammatic poems written by Nickson over the past seven decades are here collected under the title *Stones.* There are a few bouquets, but for the most part zinging brickbats are flying. The poems in free and metrical verse range widely in subject matter, intention, and tone.